The Language of

Lust

- How to Dirty Talk Your Way into His Heart • Become His Sexual Obsession • Make Your Wildest Fantasies Come True... •

By Eric Monroe

Table of Contents

Untwist Your Tongue

Sweet whispered nothings that send a shiver down his spine. Long, drawn out sentences that paint a picture of exactly what you would like to be doing to your man right at this moment, right here, and how you would like to be doing it.

Talking dirty can be a delicious boost to your romantic encounters that is guaranteed to get your man going like few other things can and will make every single orgasm you experience more powerful than ever before.

I'm not exaggerating, it really is going to make that much of a difference to your sex life – opening the pages of this book is the single best decision you've ever made for your libido. Everything about how you communicate your desires, how you push the limits of intimacy in your relationship and how you get your man's motor running is about to change.

But there's a problem here that we're going to need to address. You're here because you want to expand your sexual repertoire and take your time spent between the sheets to brand new levels. You're also here because you don't know how and you're not actually sure if you have it in you to do it – right?

Of course you do, but I understand your thinking. Few things in this world can make a woman cringe like the mention of "dirty talk" – it's still the best kept secret the boudoir ever had, even in these enlightened times when a confident woman who owns her sexuality with pride is the holy grail for all those men worth dating. Even if you already know that it has the power to elevate your love making to new heights, something about pillow talk almost certainly makes you twitch.

So what's the problem here? And, as a relationship counselor who's also had some mind blowing encounters with women who are able to wield dirty whispers like they're a weapon of mass seduction, why do I see so much reluctance to try a little sexy talk in the women I work with?

For the most part, as far as I can tell, women see sex talk as either something to be feared, something to be hidden or something that you simply feel you couldn't possibly ever pull off. It's words you can't imagine yourself saying and sentences you can't imagine yourself composing. Because of this, up until now, it's made you uneasy even thinking about it, so it got quietly packed into the corner, never to be seen again. Until now, that is.

So here's the rub of it: we all know that talking dirty can be the exquisite cherry on top of the sexual cake. A lot of us would love to have that talent – right here, right now, without any effort at all, and without the need to try and fail along the way. That's why you're here, reading this page, is it not?

But we also know it takes practice to get that language of love just right, and we are painfully aware that the practice itself has the potential to be one of the most humiliating experiences of our lives. One slip up and we just can't get over the fear that we'll become a laughing stock, sniggered about in locker rooms for years to come.

It's true, I will grant you, that those first few naughty sentences that you allow to slip through your pouting lips aren't likely to win any awards, but everyone has to start somewhere. Only the biggest asshole would mock you if you went wrong, and here's the big secret that I know is going to spur you on to give this dirty talking business a go...

...It's sexy even when it's not perfect.

Go ahead, read that sentence again, just to cement it into your mind. If you're worried that dirty talk is always going to be just out of your reach because you're too shy, embarrassed or reserved to give it a serious try, then that sentence is your key.

Trust me: as a man, I can tell you that the very act of talking dirty is a turn on. It doesn't have to be pitch perfect, it can actually be pure and unadulterated nonsense and it's still going to flip his trigger.

Why? Because there really is nothing more attractive than a woman who exudes confidence from every pore – who isn't afraid to tell her man what she wants and how she wants it.

In this guide, I'm going to turn you into that woman. More accurately, I'm going to coax that woman out from inside of you, where she's been hiding all this time, just waiting for you to take a deep breath and let her come forth.

You've always had the ability to whisper sweet, naughty nothings into his ear. It's just that, until this very moment, you hadn't unlocked it. So let's go ahead and do just that, shall we?

The Power of Speech: Or, Why Dirty Talk Will Change Your Life

Let's get the elephant in the room out of our way right away: we all know why it is that pillow talk gets such a bad rap. For all that we've progressed as a society over the last few decades, we still feel – very, very deep down, hidden away in a dark corner of our psyches – that there's something a little bit sinful about expressing our innermost desires.

Cultural norms take a long time to fade completely out of existence. This one in particular has been lingering at the corner of our awareness for at least as long as it has taken us to admit that parachute pants were not that great an idea after all.

Consciously, we think of ourselves as enlightened beings who understand equality of the genders and empowerment of our fellow man and yadda yadda yadda. Of course we do – we've been telling ourselves these things for twenty years. It's actually highly and pleasingly unlikely that, within your own sexual lifetime, you've ever encountered a sexual partner who has overtly judged you for your behavior between the sheets.

But, subconsciously, you're still being hit by some confusing signals. Television shows and movies are still telling you that a woman in touch with her sexuality is bad on the inside (that's why the virgin never dies in a horror movie and the girl who gets frisky for the very first time is guaranteed to be next one picked out for the murderer's chopping block).

It's why magazines are defiant in their tone, selling sex poses and ways to attract a man in the type of voice a toddler uses when she thinks it's definitely not her bed time quite yet. It's why your mom still thinks you should save yourself for marriage (and probably silently thinks that you should still be saving yourself even if you've already done the marriage thing).

We're getting there, but we're not there yet. Actually, you wouldn't be wrong to think of yourself as a sexual suffragette by setting out on this journey – a pioneering spirit who's helping to usher in the true age of sexual enlightenment.

Or you might just think of yourself as a sexually healthy woman who would like a little added dash of spice in her relationships and the confidence to go out right now and get it. You are both, so whichever one you prefer to call yourself is entirely up to you.

The trouble with dirty talk is all in the name: it's something we associate with kinky boudoir behavior and outspoken sexuality. It's something we can't help but think of as belonging to sex professionals and the type of girl who was whispered about in high school as "an easy lay" or "the class bike".

It's such a shame that we're living in a time when all this is pinging around inside our skulls. I, for one, think it's time that we let go of all the taboos and embrace the idea that sexuality is a part of our lives that we'd be foolish to do anything but embrace.

So why am I such a huge proponent of sexy talk? It's not just because of the boost it can give to your intimacy levels with your partner. It's not just because of the ways it can trigger your pleasure centers. It's not even just because it can thrill your man to the point that he's begging to please be allowed to please you.

Dirty talk has all these benefits and many more. Let's look at some of them in more detail:

- Talking in general is never a bad thing – communication is, as you've heard a million times, the key to a healthy relationship. So why would we think that that mantra ends where the bedroom door opens? Your man is not a mind reader – he can't always tell what you want from him between the sheets. Even a guy who is listening for every moan and watching every movement can read the signals wrong, but pillow talk is a great way to put him back on track.

- Speaking of getting your guy on track, we all know that some girls are harder to please than others. It's just a fact of life – some women will orgasm only if you find their g spot, others are guaranteed a climax as soon as their clitoris is touched. Some need a particular type of action, others need to be stimulated with a hand or a tongue rather than a penis. There's nothing even remotely wrong with this – but there is something wrong with not feeling that you're able to tell your man about what you need. Mastering the art of sexy talk can help you overcome the inhibitions or worries that are stopping you from doing that.

- Whispering new ideas in your man's ear while you're in the middle of a steamy encounter is a much easier way to break the ice than bringing it up over breakfast. "Hey, honey, I feel like trying anal beads. Pass the eggs?" Context is key if you're a shy kinda girl who isn't sure how to approach these kinds of conversations. If you're already both heavy breathing, anything goes – and especially if you've grown used to sharing your fantasies with each other.

- We'll talk about role play in more detail later, but suffice to say that bringing in a little imagination to your bedroom activities can really spice things up. You could still be doing the same five-minute-foreplay-missionary-then-finish-with-a-doggystyle-climax you've done a thousand times if that's what gets you off best, but what about adding in a touch of naughty waitress action to change the atmosphere? You'll be surprised just how much it could turn you both on.

- One of the key aspects of pillow talk is that it requires you to open up and share thoughts that you may never have thought you'd be brave enough to share. Even telling your dude that you like his hand just there or you want him to go slow and hard are things that the average woman might think would be excruciating, if she hadn't had the benefit of learning the tricks of this trade. Now imagine

13

that you feel completely comfortable sharing those thoughts with your partner. Imagine how close the two of you would then feel to one another – isn't that a goal it's well worth aiming for?

- Sexy talk can seriously pump up the anticipation. Let's imagine for a second that your lover is away for the weekend and you can't wait for him to get back home so that you can sweep him off your feet. You can tell him that – and you can tell him all those kinky little details of what you're imagining. By the time you're both in the same room, you'll be wired enough to skip the foreplay part altogether.

- Sex talk can make you more adventurous. All those hidden desires you've considered in passing, all those things you've heard about but never had the confidence to try will now be yours for the taking. Things that your man has dreamed of that you've never heard of at all, new ideas that arise as you're in the midst of all that passion. It's not just the best way to explore your sexual desires together with your lover, it's also the ONLY way. Again with the communication: only if you're telling each other what's in your heart can you truly come together in more physical ways.

You had an inkling that dirty talk could be important to your relationship – that's why you're here, reading this chapter. But you might not have realized that it's, in my opinion, the single most profound change that you'll ever make to your sex life.

What's coming up in the next few chapters is as true an interpretation of the phrase "sexual awakening" as you'll ever encounter. Mastering this skill isn't just going to titillate your guy or make you feel more comfortable to let him know that he's rubbing round the wrong hole. It's going to change everything about your sex life – and I really do mean everything.

Ready to find out how? Then let's begin...

Setting Up Your Ground Rules

While the whole idea of sexy talk made you uncomfortable until you bit the bullet and decided it was time to invite something new into your love life, there are still some potential pitfalls that I would like to help you avoid. It's all about boundaries – and by that, I mean it's about what you like, what you don't like and what you're prepared to try.

I want us to think about this a little before we dive in to the real nitty gritty of this topic. Why? Because it's important that you establish and follow your personal ground rules along the way.

Dirty talk can get out of hand, no matter whether you're sending him a text message or you're both groaning in those last beautiful throes of an orgasm. There is a possibility that you might be willing to go further in those moments than you would in the cold light of day.

I never want you to regret what you're doing here, and there really is no reason you ever should. I want this to be one of the most incredible experiences of your life, so I want you to be safe along the way.

The best way to remove those possible pitfalls, you see, is to see them coming. To decide before you whisper a single syllable exactly what your sexual boundaries really are.

For example, let's answer a few questions. Think about these now, while you're sober, and you'll have your answer when the passion kicks in and your decisions are being driven by something very different to logic:

- **Are there any sex acts you would be absolutely unwilling to perform?** Panting out those inner desires during a steamy session doesn't equate to agreeing that you'll rush straight out and make sure they happen, but it's worth bearing in mind that you might want to avoid your personal no go zones. If the idea of a golden shower activates your gag reflex, it might not be a topic you should bring up during your sex talk. At least at first, until you and your partner have established your own rules for your pillow talk and you know beyond doubt that he won't take your fantasy role play as an invitation to actually do what you're discussing, steer away from anything that makes you feel uncomfortable.

- How interested are you in the idea of role play? Role play is a pretty general term for something that can run the gamut from suggesting you get down and dirty in a public place to acting out an entire scene while wearing costumes and wielding props. Most role play partners start small and explore together until they hit their barriers, so as long as you trust your partner you'll have a heck of an adventure together. But before you do, think about topics that could leave you feeling cold. Maybe you love the idea of domination, for instance, or maybe it makes you feel uncomfortable. Maybe you'd love to be the naughty school girl, or maybe that's on your taboo list. Once you feel comfortable enough to bring these things up in conversation, you might want to think about sharing those taboo topics with your partner so that he knows to steer clear of them and it doesn't kill the mood when he accidentally touches on something you're not up for and you're forced to find a way to shut him down.

- Would you be willing to allow your significant other to own naked images of you? If you're horrified at that thought right now, don't let the momentum wash you along towards making a decision you'll regret. If he asks for a picture of you wearing the lingerie he loves best and you have no qualms with the idea of him keeping that image on his phone, then go ahead – nothing wrong with knowing he's got your curves on back up when he's away from you, if that's what turns you on. But if you balk at the idea now, you'll balk even harder after you've gone ahead and hit the send button.

One quick addendum before we move on: bear in mind, please, that your sexuality is not a solid beast. It's fluid and constantly changing, both with age and with experience.

What you like and dislike right now might not be the same as what you prefer when you've explored some more with your lover, particularly as one of the biggest advantages of mastering sexy talk is that it widens your sexual horizons. Be open to those changes and revisit these questions along the way, just to check that your answers are still the same.

A Word at a Time: How to Start Your Seduction

You're probably thinking that talking dirty is all well and good in theory, but where are you supposed to start? You have no idea how your man is going to react when you let loose with your lips, especially if you're a new couple or you've been together for years and years without either of you ever having said a word in bed.

So what's the first thing you should say? How should you introduce the idea of sex talk into your lives without worrying about the embarrassment factor? And how can you include him in this journey with you if you know that pillow talk is as new a concept to him as it is to you?

Your first step is to get comfortable with the language of love. These are words and phrases you don't necessarily use in day to day life and they will feel strange at first as they roll off your tongue. You'll need to be able to use words like "cock", "wet", "hard", "fuck me" and "tight" in a new context with ease, so I want you to start using them right now – but, before you use them with an audience, just to yourself. Try whispering phrases like, "fuck me harder", "bend over" and "come in me right now". Get used to hearing them in your own voice – practice the tone you want to use and the diction. Keep going until you can say "pussy" as easily as you can say "cupcake".

Now, we're going to start introducing sexy talk into your conversations. Because it's easier on the ego, we're going to start by using the written word – and you're going to find this a breeze now you've grown used to using much steamier words than you'll be starting with.

I want you to email, message or text your man with a conversation starter. You're going to use this to encourage him to open up – to test the waters to see exactly how prepared he is to engage in some dirty talk. He might not be very good at it yet, but I can almost guarantee you'll pique his interest right away, so you're bound to at least get an enthusiastic response. Believe me, there are very few men whose ears (and other parts) don't prick up when their women start whispering dirty thoughts.

Here are a few ideas for some of those conversation starters – use one of them or come up with your own, if they spark an idea. Pick one now to begin with, then start to use these more and more often in your text conversations. You'll notice that the list gets steamier the further down you go, so pick a comfort level and then begin to escalate as you go along.

When you're ready, you can switch to speaking these questions out loud – just make sure that you've got an hour or so free to be dragged into the bedroom and thrown down on the mattress when you do.

- What turns you on the most about a woman?
- If you could dress me up in anything right now, what would it be?
- Where's the sexiest place you've ever made love?
- What's the hottest thing a woman has ever done for you?
- Do you prefer it when I ride you or when you take me from behind?
- I want to do one thing in bed for you that we've never done before. Your choice: what should it be?
- What do you think about when you're getting yourself off?
- When you fantasize about me, what do you see?
- What's the naughtiest thing you've ever wanted to do in bed?

- If I was there right now and totally naked, what would you do to me first?
- I'm blindfolded, tied up and at your mercy. What are you gonna do to me?

Keep reading the next chapter only once you've got things rolling. It may be right away or perhaps it's going to happen over the course of a few days or even weeks, one question at a time and gradually getting steamier over time.

Don't worry if you need a little easing into the swing of things, there's no hurry. And don't worry if your man is a bit slower to react than you expected. Remember that he might be a novice too and not sure how to carry on this particular conversation. It doesn't mean he doesn't want to, it just means he has the same barriers that you did before you picked up this book.

Ready to move on? The answer is yes if you're loving every minute and you're already way wetter than you expected to be. You're waiting for his next message, staring at your phone, tingling just a little between the thighs, and you're raring to take this to the next stage.

So shall we take this conversation somewhere a little more private?

The Sounds of Pleasure – and How to Use Them

The moment you've been simultaneously anticipating and dreading has arrived. You're getting hot and heavy in person with your honey, you've tested the waters and made sure that he knows you want to include some verbal seduction into your sex life together and you know now that you definitely enjoy it when you do.

This is the first time, though, that you're going to share those words with him out loud. The first time they're going to be audible in your own voice. It's a small step from flirting on instant messenger to uttering a few words of encouragement in the bedroom, but it's also one that looks huge when you're standing on this side of it.

That's why I want you to start out nice and small. We're not going to jump right in there and start crafting erotic stories for you to tell. We're just going to add a few words here and there during your lovemaking and concentrate mostly on simply making sounds.

If you're wondering what effect this is going to have on your man in and of itself, let me reassure you: it's going to drive him wild. The reason for this is purely biological.

On a deep and instinctual level, your man knows that you are more likely to conceive a baby if you orgasm. Now, I know you're not actually in this to start saving up for a college fund and I hope you're using plenty of protection to make sure that doesn't happen – but your bodies aren't on the same page.

Sex being a biological imperative, we're wired to do it in quantities and ways that are most likely to help us procreate. When you're moaning, you are also strongly signaling that you are enjoying what your man is doing, which he interprets as meaning that he's successfully pleasing you.

Moaning and making a few noises essentially tells him that, yes, he's going to be making you throw your head back in pleasure any moment now. It doesn't just give him an ego boost on a conscious level – it's telling him that he's doing a great job on every level imaginable.

Let's pause for a second before we beckon him between the sheets: if you'd like some practice on your own before you let him hear you in all your moaning glory, then you can do that just as easily as you can climax without him present. Yep, I'm talking about masturbation.

Find yourself a private place where you're not going to be overheard, lock the door to guarantee you won't be interrupted, crank up the music if you're still a little squeamish at the idea of listening to yourself and, when you're ready, work your magic and practice rewarding yourself with sounds of pleasure as you climb towards orgasm.

The key, you see, is to mean every noise you make. You can't fake these sounds very easily, they're going to need to be genuine reactions to the sensations you're experiencing. By giving this a go in private, you can feel free to vocalize in whatever way comes most naturally to you and you'll know what to expect when you do this with an audience.

So give it a try and let whatever happens happen. Some women feel most comfortable sticking to pure moans from start to finish. Others find themselves pouring out whole sentences or strings of expletives, others call out to their deities while in the throes of pure passion. Remember that it isn't important what your sounds of pleasure are: it just matters that you develop the confidence to let them out.

Now let's return to the bedroom, where your man is poised waiting to make sure you enjoy yourself. He already knows that something is a little bit different after all those juicy messages you've been sending him. It's time to coax him to the next level alongside you – and you're going to do that by rewarding his ego and his subconscious with those beautiful moans.

Again, let's start small and grow in confidence. Here are some ideas as to what you might try to get you started. You can trust when I say that this part is going to come naturally, but having these ideas already unlocked in your mind can only boost that confidence:

- "Mmmm", "uhhhh" and other simple moans
- "Oh my god"
- "Yes!"
- "Oh baby"
- "Oh baby, don't stop"
- "Oh god that feels good"
- "Oh god, harder"
- "Yes, right there"
- "Oh keep going"

See? Simple. But let's talk about what's happening on the other side of the equation: how is your man reacting?

Again, everyone is different, so how exactly he reacts to your newfound primal instincts will depend on his personality. Some reactions will seem to be more encouraging than others but, unless he flat out tells you that he didn't like it when you moaned (and, believe me, the chances of that are virtually nonexistent), you shouldn't ever take it as disapproval.

Some guys will respond instantly, moaning right back at you with utter abandon. Others may seem shocked and surprised at what you're doing, especially if you've been together a long time and it's been silence up until this moment. Still others may be spurred on to thrust harder and faster than ever before, completely losing control, while others will be silent at first but then tentatively start giving their own low moans.

All of these reactions are perfectly normal. Bear in mind that you've just completely and unexpectedly altered the dynamic of your sexual partnership, and that can come as a surprise during the first encounter.

He might even ask you about it, if he's the curious type. Maybe he'll want to know what on earth it was he did to you this time that he's never managed to do before. Obviously you don't need to tell him you picked up this book and you're going through the learning stages, though you're free to do that if you want to. I'd recommend something instead that you can say with a wink and a smile, such as, "I just feel comfortable enough with you now to let my true self roar" or, "I don't know, it just happened and then it felt so right."

Now you've made that connection, you can continue to use your sounds of seduction as you enjoy one another between the sheets. There's no hurry to move on from this point – indeed, some couples are happy to stick right here and never take things to the next level at all.

But, after a while, I'm willing to bet that you're going to find yourself thinking about stepping up your game and wondering how far you could take things and just how pleasurable it might get. So, in the next chapters, we're going to look at different types of sexy talk and what effect they're going to have on you, your man and your sex life.

You can try them all, if you want to – the sky is very much the limit at this point. I would suggest that you read through these chapters and pick the one that appeals to you the most at this very moment. Start there, and then see where the passion takes you next.

1. Dirty Talk to Seduce Your Man

You can use a little tongue action to turn your man on far before you ever hit the pillow, turning a regular date or day together at home into a panting, sweaty tangle of limbs. By using dirty talk to seduce your man into bed, what you're actually doing is taking control of the when, where and how the encounter plays out. You are becoming the dominant partner, just for a little while, by using your sexy talk as a seduction tool.

Why?
Let's say that you're in a long term relationship and the sex isn't as frequent as it used to be, or that your guy doesn't seem to have a particularly high libido and that means he doesn't think to initiate sex nearly as often as you'd like him to. Or maybe this is the first time you've seduced this particular man into bed and you want to start things out with a bang.

Maybe it's just that he's usually the instigator when it comes to initiating sex and the idea of changing things round really tingles your toes. Or perhaps you don't feel as though you're quite as in control of your sex life as you ought to be and you want to use your newfound skills to change that. Or maybe you just feel like surprising him with a sexual encounter he really wasn't expecting...

When?

Pick your timing well for the very best results. You're going to want a relatively long lead up time before the two of you can actually come together physically, but you will need to be in constant communication during that time.

There's not much point turning him on just before an eight hour plane journey, for example, when the communication gap is way too long to sustain the anticipation you're hoping to inspire. You'll also get good results if you're saying these things in person when it won't be possible to actually meet pelvises until later on – otherwise, this whole thing is going to come to a head a lot more quickly than we want it to.

Plus, of course, you're going to want to be able to really enjoy yourselves once your sexy talk comes to fruition, so make sure you'll have some decent time together in private once things do come to a head. I also recommend trying this out for the first time on a special occasion so it doesn't quite come out of the blue, if that would make you feel more comfortable. Make it a birthday present to remember or a Valentine that meets his every desire.

How?

Think of this as a process that's much the same as when you tested the waters by messaging him flirty texts at the very beginning – only, this time, you have a solid goal in mind and you've increased your confidence levels and made sure both of you know how sexy talk works within your relationship.

We're going to start by surprising him with a question that's dirtier and more intriguing than you've ever asked before. Take charge of this right away and never let go of those reins.

You can either message him this question if you've chosen to do this at a time when you're apart (and there really is something extra exciting about naughty messages when you're surrounded by people in the workplace or a public space) or ask him out loud if you're together

Try something along the lines of:

- "Do you know what I'm wearing underneath these clothes?"
- "Tell me which part of my body you find the sexiest"
- "If I got naked right now, what would you do?"

- "What do you wish you could be doing to me right now?"
- "If I went down on you right now, could you stay quiet?"
- "I'm thinking about what we did at the weekend. If I told you I was wet just thinking of you, what would you do?"
- "What are we gonna do about the fact that I want you inside me so badly I'm trembling?"
- "I had a naughty dream about you last night. Do you want to know what I did to you?"

Notice that each of these questions requires a response. He can't grunt an answer or nod and smile – he has to join in with the conversation.

There's a reason for this. You're jump starting a dialogue that you could easily keep up for hours at a time, pushing things further and sexier until you have the opportunity to get in each other's pants.

You'll want to respond to whatever he says naturally, with the response that you really are thinking. If you find that the conversation is trailing off, try another question to get it going again. Try to escalate things – start peppering your responses with the words you're now comfortable using. Tell him that you can't wait to lick his cock, whisper that you want him to fuck you harder than he ever has before, let him know that your pussy has been waiting for him all day.

The queens of seduction can pull this off for hours, sometimes even days, stringing their man along and keeping him panting with anticipation that's as exciting and effective as physical foreplay.

For your first try, though, you may want to limit the time between that first question and the moment you both get what you need. Right now, neither of you are used to playing the waiting game.

There's a delicate balance between stringing out that desire and reaching a point where it stops being interesting because, consciously, you've worked out that you can't get satisfaction. So start this process just a few hours before the two of you can get each other alone.

Alternatively, take him out for the evening on a date and start the conversation over the dinner table – if it gets to a point where you know in your heart and loins that you really need to get those clothes peeled off, you can call it an early evening and head back home.

2. Dirty Talk to Keep the Sexual Tension Going

The kind of couple who has real chemistry is the kind of couple that can bring sex into almost any aspect of their lives. They use lovemaking as a reward, a way to connect and a way to maintain their intimacy, as well as a joyous method to simply spend some quality time together. You've probably met one of these couples – they're the ones that make you think, "oh for goodness sake, get a room", because their connection is obvious no matter what they're doing. You can use your verbal seduction tools to bring that into your own relationship.

Why?

That desperate need to touch your lover is something that can fade over time thanks to good old fashioned over familiarity. It's almost as though we got what we wanted and now we're bored and looking for something new to excite us – and that can sometimes be a new sexual partner, to recapture the magic. That's bad news for your relationship, obviously. The down side of this fact, you see, is that it lessens your intimacy with each other over time, if you allow it to happen.

By utilizing dirty talk, however, you can make sure that the sexual tension never leaves your relationship. There's nothing to stop you from keeping it bubbling until you're both on walkers and more interested in whether there'll be gravy with your meals on wheels delivery than you are in getting frisky.

The reason it's such a powerful tool is that it invokes our innate desire to chase and catch our sexual prey. Men in particular have this drive – you might have it too, or you might be wired to enjoy being chased. Either way, activating the chase is something that will keep both of you thinking about each other's touch and taste even when you're stood together at the sink, finishing the washing up.

When?

This particular dirty talk style can literally be used at any moment of any day – that's the whole point. You're changing the dynamic of your relationship to make sure that sex is a factor at all times and that you're always, at the back of your mind, thinking about what your partner looks like naked.

All you need to do is insert sex into the questions and conversations you're already having. It's easy and it's fun – but it might take a little bit of practice.

How?

For this one, I want you to spend a little time thinking about your daily lifestyle and coming up with some tantalizing little tidbits that will add a dash of sex to the routine.

To demonstrate, I'm going to give you some examples to get your imagination going. Feel free to use them directly, as always, but feel just as free to replace them with your own ideas:

- Instead of saying, "Honey, would you mind cleaning the bathroom," try, "Baby, I want you to go get as dirty as that bathroom is and then I'm gonna come clean you."

- Instead of saying, "Baby could you grab some milk and eggs from the store," try, "Here's your list – the quicker you get to the cash register, the faster you'll know whether I'm here waiting for you completely naked."

- Instead of asking, "When do you think you'll be home tonight?", ask him, "How fast can you get here? I have a surprise for you..."

- Throw some sex based compliments into the mix. Let him know that he looks good enough to bite in that shirt and that you might just do exactly that when he gets home from work. Tell him you're seriously considering skipping out on the dinner party because you'd rather be tasting his skin.

- Be flirty, as though this is a guy you're confident enough to approach in a crowded bar even though you have no way to know if he wants to get up close and personal with him. Lock your eyes on his and ask him what he's doing later, tell him you couldn't help but notice him looking at your ass and you wondered if he'd like to see it more closely.

Starting to get the idea? Give him some little thrills of excitement and it won't just be him casting sidelong glances at the bedroom door – you'll both be thinking constantly about how much fun you know you can have together.

3. Dirty Talk to Get a Commitment From Your Man

I've helped more women who can't seem to get a commitment out of their man than I can count, and this is the solution I always recommend first. It takes a bit of effort, but you have an advantage over those clients of mine: you've already laid the groundwork by making it this far into the book.

This method will help you show your man that he's missing out and should be making this relationship exclusive right away.

Why?

Some relationships can go on for years without any firm commitment from one or both of you. If you're thinking of trying out this method, it means that the commitment shy half of the partnership is him – and that you're looking for a way to make up his mind for him.

If this method doesn't work, you'll still be glad you tried it. It's going to tell you whether the dude is worth your time because it's either going to work like a charm, or it's going to reveal that he's simply unable or unwilling to commit to you. It's the acid test you've been searching for, and it all comes down to your sex talk.

When?

Obviously you don't want to rush into this one. If you've only been dating a few weeks, he probably is genuine in not being willing to make a commitment yet. Use your common sense and good judgment to decide when the time is right. You've been together for many months or a few years, you know each other on a deep level and you're spending most of your free time together, but he doesn't seem willing to make it official.

How?

First up, you're going to back off from him a little bit and make him start to miss you. Don't be available as much as you have been, find a few new hobbies to occupy your time and cut dates short before you let him get his way with you. Doing this makes him start to see you as something he must strive for and earn rather than something that automatically belongs to him.

The next step is where your dirty talk skills come in. I want you to use a combination of teasing him and blowing his mind in the bedroom – and I want you to do so in equal measure.

You're not going to give him what he wants every single time any more. And when you decide to deny him full satisfaction, I want you to use dirty talk to cement that decision:

- "It's time to cool this down, baby. That alarm is gonna start ringing before I know it"

- "I want you so badly, but I'm afraid this is going to have to wait for another time"

- "Mmmmm, let's stop things right here. We can pick them up again tomorrow"

Cut him short and leave him with all that unspent desire. Remove yourself from his presence and then send him a flirty text to really drive the point home.

- "Feel free to think of me while you finish yourself off ;)"

- "I guess I'll be seeing you in your dreams a little later ;)"

Now, this isn't going to work if he's not getting the most out of the sex you are letting him have. You want him to think of getting you naked as the greatest reward of his life.

That's easily done, now you know how: muster all that new found confidence and talk as dirty as you dare. Tell him not to stop until he's come so hard he can't breathe, tell him to watch as you cum for him, demand that he fucks you raw and that he moans for you all the while he does it. Drive him wild with desire – tell him to fuck you from behind, purr that you love his cock so much, let him know that he's driving you crazy. Pump up the volume on your sex talk as high as you dare.

Final stage. Now we're going to make him feel loved and appreciated – and not necessarily for what he can do with his cock. Tell him, out loud or via a message, that you love, admire, respect or value him and precisely why. Maybe it's his work ethic or his good manners, perhaps it's the way he is with his family, his sense of humor even in sticky situations or the care he takes of the way he looks.

Whatever you choose, make sure you mean it – he'll know it if you don't. You'll stroke his ego because all men love to know that their woman appreciates them and has noticed the efforts they've made.

That's all there is to it. By bringing dirty talk into the equation, you've shown him that you're a woman worth chasing and that he's going to get plenty of rewards from doing exactly that. A few simple sentences and you're going to get the commitment you've been working for all this time.

4. Dirty Talk to Free Your Inhibitions

If you walked around with a clipboard and pen and asked every guy you know what one thing they would change about their woman in bed, at least half of them would say the same thing: they would love her to show more enthusiasm. That doesn't mean you're a vegetable who lays back and thinks of England, before you think I'm insulting your technique. It just means that he wants you to forget about absolutely everything else and concentrate on what's happening between you right here and right now.

Why?

Even if you love everything about sex and you can barely wait to rip your man's clothes off when you get home from work, it's all too easy to get distracted when naked time actually comes around. Women worry that their stomach isn't flat enough, that there isn't a big enough gap between their thighs, that they aren't as good at this as his ex, that they look silly in this position, that they might make some perfectly natural but pretty funny noises if he angles in just such a way, that he isn't enjoying himself – you name it, I've worked with a woman who thought it.

For the guy in this equation, it can dampen the mood. He's not thinking about your thighs or your belly, he was turned on enough by you that you're here in the first place and that isn't going to change. He's not comparing you to anyone or worrying about the natural noises of sex, he just wants to get down and dirty and enjoy every moment you're alone.

He wants you to do that too. And if you can, it will heighten the enjoyment for the both of you.

When?
As soon as you possibly can. This particular dirty talk application is designed much more for you than it is for him – you're the one who is suddenly going to experience a whole new world of pleasure, but his added enjoyment is definitely a bonus. The sooner you bite the bullet and give it a go, the sooner you'll be upping the ante on your sex life.

How?
Start by making a few small changes that will make you feel more comfortable. Dim the lights a little more than usual, put on some music in the background so the silence is less deafening, make sure the curtains are closed and your phone is on silent.

Now put that practice you've been doing into action. Purr some noises as things start heating up, let yourself get into the rhythm. Meanwhile, I want you to close your eyes and concentrate absolutely on the sensations you are feeling. The way he's making you feel, what his skin feels like against you and under your fingertips.

Now, as the foreplay gets hotter, I want you to think about what it's going to feel like when he slips inside you – and I want you to tell him how much you want that to happen.

As always, some ideas for you to roll around your tongue ahead of time and either use exactly as I've written them or adapt to suit your own style:

- "You fuck me so good, I want you inside me right now"

- "I can't wait any longer, I want to feel you fill me up"

- "My pussy is your toy, baby, it's all yours. Do whatever you want to it, just do it right now"

- "Please, please fuck me – I need you inside me"

- "Fuck me so hard it hurts, baby, I want to feel you deep inside me"

- "Oh god you feel so good. I need you inside me right now"

- "Do you want to fuck me? Feel my tight pussy? I want that so bad, just take it"

- "Fuck me any way you want to, I'm yours for the taking"

Keep going as he enters you – keep your eyes closed and your attention completely on those amazing sensations. What you've done so far will have driven him wild so expect to be fucked harder than he's fucked you in the past.

Letting these sentences slip out of your mouth automatically lowers your inhibitions. It's as though your words break through those barriers that you've put up and allow you to connect with him on a level you couldn't before.

Now you can either revert back to the noises you were making, interspersed with a lot of "oh god" and "oh yes, yes, that feels so good", or you can continue to dirty talk him to orgasm:

- "Don't stop, oh god don't stop, I'm gonna cum so hard"

- "You know exactly what my pussy needs, don't stop"

- "Oh god yes, right there, that feels so damn good"

- "This feels so good I don't ever want it to stop"

- "I'm gonna cum for you baby, can you feel that"

By the time you're spent, you'll be wondering why you ever stayed silent – and a whole new world of sex will have opened up before you. After all, isn't everything more fun when you don't have to worry about it all the way through?

5. Dirty Talk When He Can't Get It Up

Very few things have the power to destroy a healthy relationship faster than impotence. Whether it's because you're the hottest woman he's ever met and he's so nervous he can't get it up; he's going through a period of ill health or high stress and it's affecting his performance; or he has a long term problem that may have no solution, it can leave you feeling unattractive and unwanted.

Fortunately, this little magic spell we call dirty talk can really help in all these situations. It might not create an instant erection, but it can certainly keep the two of you steamy and passionate despite the setback.

Why?

All the reasons that impotence might happen can be linked by one sad fact: when he can't get it up, it eventually erodes the intimacy between the two of you. Dirty talk has two slightly different functions in this case, however, so let's talk about them one by one.

- If you've just reached the stage where you're inviting him home for coffee only for a disappointment when you reach down between his legs, the reason is probably nerves.

Maybe it's because he's so attracted to you that he's terrified he might disappoint, maybe he's had a bad experience in the past. If you're prepared to tell him how much you want him and guide him towards pleasing you, you'll be surprised how quickly that problem melts away.

- If the two of you have been together for a while and have never experienced anything like this before, it could be illness, tiredness or stress. Something has changed and, despite where your mind will instantly go, it probably isn't anything to do with you. Assuming it's not, what can you do to make things better? Simple. You can create the same levels of intimacy in different ways, guiding him through your dirty talk into pleasing you in brand new ways and enjoying himself in return. And who knows, if it's not a permanent problem, you might find a little someone standing to attention along the way.

When?
In the first scenario we just discussed, you'll know right away if you need to put your guy at ease through a little pillow talk. Catch him before his

anxiety reaches peak levels – as soon as you realize he might be facing a problem.

Don't leave an awkward silence, instantly purr something that's both understanding and sexy, such as, "Mmmmm, I'm just gonna have to work a little harder to convince both of you I'm worth a try". Wink and smile to put him at his ease and let him know you understand and aren't judging him in any way. These things happen, right?

In the second scenario, you might want to think about talking to your man about the problem and letting him know there's plenty of fun you could be having without his penis even factoring in. If he's game to try, you can direct him through the process and help him feel comfortable all along the way.

How?

Let's once again start with the first scenario. You've let him know you understand, now you just need to show him that you are prepared to take things slow until he's ready and that you definitely still want him. Make sure you're making all sorts of encouraging noises when he touches you in the right places. Give him a thrill as you do, let him realize just what a dirty girl he's playing with. Try something along the lines of:

- "Want to feel just how wet I am for you already? Here, give me your hand and let me show you"

- "I've been waiting for this moment all day. Thinking about how your skin would feel rubbing against mine"

- "I want you to taste me – why don't you lick my pussy and see how much it wants you"

- "You could do anything you wanted with my body and I would moan for you"

- "I've been thinking about getting you naked since the day we first met. I want to touch every inch of your skin"

Keep the conversation directed away from his penis – right now, telling him you want him to cum inside you is adding insult to injury. Focus on the things you could be doing. Let him explore your body and encourage him to do that in just the right way to make you moan. Don't worry – it's not selfish. You're showing him that the problem doesn't matter, you still want him and he can still keep his ego intact by pleasing you just fine.

Sooner or later, those nerves are going to dissipate. He's going to relax in your naked company and forget that he was worried about his performance. Direct him to do things that will make you orgasm and watch his reaction – I bet it will be a stiff one.

Moving on to the second scenario, the principles are very much the same. You want your man to know that you want him and that he can please you no matter what his biology is doing to him.

Set aside a good chunk of time to get frisky together and direct what happens from start to finish. Remember that your aim here is to maintain that intimacy between you and show him that you are not put off by his problem – quite the contrary, you still want him and need him in your life.

Explore each other's bodies completely. Lay him back and kiss or lick him from head to toe, in places he hasn't been touched in a good long while. Massage him, pay a little attention to his balls with your tongue – make him tingle from top to bottom. Take this very slowly and whisper encouragement as you do, to let him know that you want to be doing this and it's a lovemaking act of its own, not a replacement.

- "I forgot just how good your skin tastes"

- "I want to commit every last inch of you to my memory so I can picture you when I daydream"

- "I could touch you all day long"

- "I love watching you lay back and enjoy my touches, it makes me feel so good"

The second important component here is, again, to make sure he knows he can still please you. Use some of the sentences I included above to direct him as well as something along these lines:

- "Remember when you made me cum while we were driving to dinner that time? I think about that a lot and it still drives me wild – will you touch me that way right now?"

- "Nobody has ever licked my pussy like you do. I want to feel you down there right now"

- "I've always wondered what it would be like to cum all over your fingers. Wanna show me?"

You're reminding him how much he's always pleased you while giving him ways to do exactly the same thing right now. That's going to boost his confidence and help him let go of some of the misery associated with losing such an important tool in his masculine kit.

Remember, I can't guarantee that you'll solve the impotence problem using dirty talk – not without knowing what caused it in the first place and whether it's reversible or permanent. What I can guarantee is that you'll maintain and perhaps increase the intimacy between you, and I think we can agree that's the most important result of all.

6. Dirty Talk When You're Far Apart

Over my years as a relationship counselor, I've worked with a lot of couples who spend a great deal of time apart. One of them works away on a regular basis, one of them travels to take care of an elderly family member, the two of them don't live in the same city yet, one of them is deployed in the military – there are all sorts of things that can create distance.

The problem with creating distance, of course, is that it becomes difficult to maintain the kind of relationship that both of them want. In other words, it becomes difficult to have sex.

Or does it?

Why?

We have a tendency to think of sex as one particular thing: the act of a cock meeting a pussy. At the very least, we think of it as something that definitely requires both parties to be in the same space at the same time. The women I've worked with in particular have told me that long distance sex couldn't possibly keep their man happy because guys just don't enjoy being swept away by erotic stories and descriptions and they're not comfortable with the idea of sending sexy images.

This is not true, and finding that out can be a massive benefit to your relationship. It can help you explore worlds together that make you desperate to rush home and find somewhere private and alone where you can really get down and dirty with your imaginations. It can help you explore each other's fantasies, likes and dislikes, which in turn is bound to make the sex mind blowing when you're back in the same city.

When?
Though you can quite literally keep a sexy conversation going for every moment that you're apart, I would recommend using this dirty talk technique relatively sparingly. Remember that you want it to be a thrilling experience and that pretty much everything gets less thrilling with repeated exposure.

You can initiate at any moment of your choosing, just be sure to bring the experience to a climax in a reasonable amount of time and to resist the temptation to start all over right away.

How?
If you've never done this before, don't worry. You don't need to pussyfoot around, you can simply dive in and get things started. Trust me when I say that

receiving a sexually charged message from you out of the blue is going to perk him up and get his blood pumping right away.

Obviously you can't really use your dirty talk verbally right now, so we're going to be relying on the means through which the two of you communicate while you're apart. Maybe that's by text message, maybe that's by email or messenger.

So send him a message that gets his mind racing, such as:

- "I had a dream about you last night and I've been wet for you all morning"

- "I keep having the same naughty thought about you and I can't get it out of my head"

- "I've been thinking about the time you stripped me naked on the hood of your car"

- "I need to fuck you"

Interest immediately piqued, right? Of course it is. Now you can lead him through a conversation. Bear in mind that men really are more straightforward than women when it comes to sexual imagery, so he's probably not going to be all that interested in a ten-page fantasy about dressing up in Victorian outfits and flirting on the balcony.

But that's ok, because you've already mastered the basics of sexy talk. You know the buzzwords that make his breathing come faster.

He's going to either ask you a curious question about where you're heading with this or he's going to immediately respond in kind. Be playful back and remember that the key is to follow his lead and continue to step things up one more step at a time as the conversation goes along.

I'm going to give you some ideas for what you might say to him during the flirting stage, some more raunchy than others. Use them according to your comfort levels. As it's likely you'll be doing this frequently until you're no longer separated (and plenty of couples keep it up even when they're not), you might just find yourself using them all:

- "If you were here right now, I'd be sliding my tongue down your chest and belly, feeling you shiver while you wonder if I'll keep going down, down, down"

- "I wish I could feel the weight of your body on top of me right and your skin hot against mine"

- "Do you know what I'm doing right now? Can you guess where my fingers are?"

- "I'm touching myself like you touch me, fingers deep inside my wet pussy"

- "I'm thinking about you bending me over and fucking me from behind and it's making me so wet"

- "If you were here and I could tear your clothes off your body, I'd drizzle you in chocolate and lick it off slowly, inch by inch"

- "I can't concentrate for thinking about you and all the things I would be doing to you right now"

- "What would you do if I just thrust my hand down the front of your pants, stroked your cock and begged you to fuck me right now?"

- "I wish you could feel how turned on I am right now. But I can at least tell you what I'm thinking about that got me this way..."

Some couples find that they enjoy swapping banter like this for hours on end and simply telling each other what they're doing to please themselves while thinking about what they'd like to be doing if they were in the same space.

Others like to guide the conversation towards a blow by blow account of the sexual encounter they wish they were having. For instance:

- "I'm sliding my tongue down your cock, sucking you hard and slow, knowing you want to grab my hair and thrust yourself into my mouth and wanting you to do it"

- "I'm gonna swallow every drop of you, then spread my legs and push your head between them. I want you to lick my clit till I moan"

- "I'm begging you to fuck me, begging for your rock hard cock inside me. I want you to spank me while you pound me hard and tell me I'm your bad girl"

Again, it all depends on your comfort levels. And when you REALLY get comfortable with this technique, there's another stage you can climb to: speaking these words out loud.

Phone sex can be intensely hot. All these words and phrases and all those descriptions of what you want to be doing to each other can be even more of a turn on out loud. Make sure you have complete privacy, put your cell on speaker phone and get to pleasuring yourself, doing the things to yourself that you wish he was doing and telling him all about it.

All those moans and groans you'll be making, the sighs of pleasure and the whispers of his name? Just imagine how much that's going to spur him on, especially knowing that you're doing this thinking of him, just like you would be if you weren't so far apart.

Still can't get enough? Why not try some video sex in this age of technological wonder. Make sure your internet connection is absolutely secure, call him up on Skype and let him see for himself how badly you want him.

Switch these things up: flirt by text one day, video fuck another day and call him on the phone some time after that. With a little imagination, you can keep your sex life just as fresh and exciting even if you're separated by hundreds of miles.

7. Dirty Talk When the Sex Isn't Great

Let's face it, sometimes even the hottest guy with the most amount of notches on his bed post isn't necessarily all that great at following through with his promises. It's not easy to tell a man that what he's doing is leaving you cold – if it was, the fake orgasm wouldn't even be a thing.

You don't want to crush his feelings, but you also don't want to spend the next 40 or so years of your life sighing in resignation whenever he slips a hand up your thigh. So let's do something about that, shall we?

Why?

Flat out saying to someone, "you're not that great in bed", is not really an option if you plan to continue getting frisky with them. At best, you're going to leave your lover panicked and anxious every time he touches you. At worst, he'll be so insulted that he won't want to try again.

By using dirty talk to guide him into understanding you and your needs, you get the best of every world. You can be as explicit as you like and as detailed as you need to be, but you're doing it in such a way that he won't just be turned on even more than ever, he'll also feel like he's constantly improving on a technique he never has to know was lacking.

When?

Be careful how you handle this one. You want to get him used to the idea of you talking dirty before you dive in with the demands, or it's going to be fairly obvious that you have an ulterior motive. Ease him into this with some murmurs and moans, start telling him how much you love it when he's inside you, call out his name.

Once you're both comfortable, you can very gradually begin to introduce guidance into the situation. I don't recommend giving him step by step instructions and it may not feel natural to do this every time you make love, so use your judgment to offer just the right amount of guidance and reward as you get to know each other.

How?

It doesn't matter what your man's specific problem in bed it. Some won't have the first clue where the important parts of your body are located, others know exactly where they are but they don't realize that your clit isn't the be all and end all of your pleasure. Some are bad kissers, others take forever to finish, while still others take you literally when you ask them to fuck you till it hurts. You'll also come across guys who have learned some really bizarre techniques they think are guaranteed to make them studs – lord only knows where they find them, but I've heard of men twisting or pinching their partner's nipples, flicking her clit and even, god help us, biting down on her most sensitive parts.

In all these situations, your task is the same: first, identify the problem. Then, decide what your very personal solution is. You can then guide him through praise of what he's already doing to do better on other things too.

Let's say he's totally ignoring everything but the goal and you wish he'd nibble your neck and go a little slower on the rest of you. Easy:

- "Oh god, I want to feel your tongue on every inch of my skin"

- "Oh my god baby, it feels so good when you do that... please keep doing it, please don't stop"

- "Follow my fingers with your lips, I want to see if you can make me tingle as much as I can"

Let's say he's taking forever to cum and you're getting sore. Whisper in his ear:

- "Cum with me baby, I want us to finish together"

What about if he's doing things completely wrong and you want him to change technique entirely? No problem, just get a bit stricter:

- "I want you to lick my pussy till I cum against your mouth"

- "Put your fingers inside me baby, make me cum for you"

- "I'm gonna tie you down and show you exactly how I want you to touch me – and then I'm gonna test you on how much you learned"

How about if he's completely silent and isn't giving you any feedback whatsoever on what YOU are doing... but you're pretty sure you're not getting it right? Ask him to show you:

- "I want you to show me how you get yourself off. I want you to cum for me and let me watch"

- "Show me where you like to be licked, let me make you feel good"

Meanwhile, you need to pepper in some encouragement so he doesn't start to feel as though he's taking an exam.

- "Oh my god, that feels so good"

- "Nobody can make me cum like you do"

- "I've never needed someone inside me like I need you right now."

As always, you're going to need to mean what you say – but that shouldn't be too hard if you're giving him the right directions to be making you feel amazing.

Using dirty talk to guide your man into pleasuring you isn't something that has to stop once you have the basics handled, either. You can use it to introduce new ideas and things that you've never tried before – in other words, you can continue to hone your sex skills together for years and years, never running out of things to say.

So if you feel like being more adventurous, start by working out your base technique. Then follow the same pattern to ask that he licks your toes, does you doggy style, fucks you in the ass, kisses your belly button or whatever else your horny self desires.

8. Dirty Talk When You Want Your Every Fantasy Fulfilled

The nuts and bolts of sex are an exquisite experience in themselves, but there's bound to come a point where you feel like experimenting – taking things a little further than you and your man have been used to. Stating out loud that you'd be interested in a threesome, getting up close and personal with him in a Navy uniform or watching porn can be intimidating. Fortunately, you can already guess before I say it that you're holding the key to sexual adventure right here in your hands.

Why?

There's no such thing as a boring sex life if the two of you are prepared to explore your boundaries. Think about it for just a second and I know you'll be able to come up with at least ten different things you'd like to try but have never had the opportunity or courage to suggest. Things like:

- Mutual oral sex in the 69 position
- Fisting
- Partner swapping or threesomes
- Positions such as doggy style

- Having sex in an unusual place, such as outdoors, in the shower, on the staircase, on a plane, at your work place
- Being watched while you make love or watching someone else
- Sex toys including handcuffs, anal beads, whips, restraints, sex swings and blindfolds
- Sex in a costume, such as a policeman, a naughty maid or a mask
- Role play where one or both of you is someone else, such as the pizza delivery guy, a burglar who gets more than he bargained for or a naughty schoolgirl
- Sex while watching yourselves in a mirror
- Bondage, domination, submission or discipline

This list could almost literally go on forever, so I'll stop here and let your mind wander a little. I want you to really think about all the ways you'd love to indulge yourself in the bedroom – write them down, if it helps.

Now you see exactly why you want to take advantage of your newfound dirty talk skills to turn your fantasies into reality. It's because you can do it without ever having to have an uncomfortable conversation you can't bring yourself to face.

When?

First up, I want to make sure you don't hurry into this one. You're going to be stretching the bounds of your sexual experience and that, in itself, has the potential to bring some anxiety to the table.

So make sure you've spent enough time getting comfortable with your sexual vocabulary before you go there. I cannot stress enough how much familiarity makes sex talk much easier to incorporate – once you've been doing it for a while, these words are going to slip easily from your mouth.

Second, I want you to prepare yourself first. Choose the fantasy you want to try out first and get things ready so you can get right to it if the mood takes. For instance, there's not much point having a handcuff fantasy and getting your man all hot and bothered to try it if you don't actually have any handcuffs available – by the time you've gone shopping to get some or had them delivered by mail, the mood is over.

In some cases that might not be possible, such as if you want him to dress up as a firefighter. If that's the case, you could be creative and, for instance, get him just the hat and turn the rest of the shopping into

71

foreplay, the both of you getting increasingly turned on as you know what's coming next.

Or perhaps you want to try out a threesome – maybe you could leave him a steamy book about it on the bedside table with a bow on it. Maybe you want to have sex in the woods – so go out there and take a teasing photo of your naked legs laying on the leaves, then text it to him with a wink.

How?

You've sowed the seeds and you're ready to give this a go, so the first thing you need to do is broach the subject. I recommend choosing a moment when the both of you are relaxed and in the mood for pillow talk – just after you've made love tends to be ideal, or while you're flirting over the internet or the phone or in a crowded restaurant where the mood has taken both of you, lowering your voice over the table to give him an idea of what you're going to do to him when you get home.

Then try something as simple as:

- "So, what's your biggest fantasy – the one you've always wanted to try?"

- "Can you guess what my biggest fantasy is? If you can, I'll let you do it to me..."

- "So if we got home tonight and you found the bedroom all set up to [insert your fantasy of choice here], what would you do?"

Once you've confirmed that he's on board, you can start exchanging ideas about it. This part is a lot like having phone or text sex: discuss the idea as though you were already there and tell each other what you'd like to do to the other and have done to you in the process. Things like:

- "If you let me tie you down and you were helpless to stop me, I'd lick every inch of you then bring you right to the edge of cumming and hold you there, begging me to keep going"

- "If you were dressed all fancy like an English butler, I'd demand you brought me chocolates and rubbed my feet, then I'd reward you by stripping that stuffy suit off you and having my way with you right there on the chaise longue"

- "I want you to fuck me in the ass, make me wet with your tongue there first and then push your cock inside slow and easy, make me gasp as you slide into me"

You might notice that, in among all the sex talk, there are some genuine notes of guidance included in what you're saying. When the time does come to indulge in this fantasy, he has a pretty good idea what you're hoping for – and you know how to make it good for him, too.

You can also build sex talk into the experience itself. Now that you're used to whispering sweet nothings and you've let go of the embarrassment that once held you back, there's nothing to stop you from play acting the scenarios that appeal to you.

Discuss this with your partner first if you think he might have some reservations, then plan a time and a place. Need some ideas to get you going? How about:

- Meet up as strangers at a local bar where nobody knows you. Agree that, just for tonight, you have no idea who the other is and you also have no reservations about hooking up with this sexy stranger who is coming on to you.

- Book a hotel room. One of you can go settle in, while the other one prepares to turn up. How you do that is up to you – wearing only a trench coat, with a sexy hooker outfit on underneath, as a forbidden fantasy arriving for a hot liaison, anything goes as long as both of you are comfortable with it.

- Greet him when he gets home from work unexpectedly dressed as a slave or servant in a sexy, revealing outfit, then proceed to obey his every command, telling him, "Yes, my king," and, "Whatever you desire, my lord". I doubt it will be very long before he orders you into the bedroom.

During most of these scenarios, you can stay almost silent if you want to – but the whole experience will be oh so very much sexier if you really get into your parts. Imagine yourself to be someone completely different, if it helps – you are an actress and, tonight, this is your role. Go with it, saying whatever feels natural.

Follow his lead if it's easier and he's more confident at this than you, or take the lead yourself and steer the conversation towards your wants and desires. By doing this, you are again subtly guiding him to please you, something that he will appreciate and is guaranteed to make your night even more spectacular.

There are countless fantasy scenarios you can play out together, it really is a case of anything you fancy. The more you do it, the easier it will become to role play as an Amazon warrior, a submissive slave or a shy librarian. Definitely the most advanced use of dirty talk on the list, this one will keep your sex life hot and steamy well into the future.

A Final Word

Congratulations – you've reached the final chapter. To get this far, you have mastered the language of lust and turned yourself from fearful to fearless – and had a whole lot of amazing sex in the process.

So let's finish this off with a few words about honing your technique over time. No matter how comfortable you feel right now with sexy talk, you can always take things further.

As you continue to try out the scenarios in this book, I want you to give yourself some time to reflect on them afterwards. Honestly and candidly ask yourself what worked well and what could go better next time.

Perhaps things were difficult over the phone and you'd feel better if you could look him in the eye. Maybe you tried out a fantasy but you got all tied up in all the wrong ways using the bondage equipment and, next time, you could stand to do a little more preparation. Or maybe you posed a new idea in a place that wasn't as comfortable as you thought for him and he turned the color of beetroot.

Use every experience as a learning opportunity and allow it to guide you as you move forward. If you find that you're losing confidence using certain words and sentences, by all means stop right there and never use them again – you've found your comfort limits and there's no need to break through them if you don't want to.

But if you do, you can return to an earlier chapter and try again. Practice those dirty words in front of the mirror, or build up to them slowly over time by aiming for some softer fantasy roleplay first.

Over time, you will begin to build a sexual repertoire that you never dreamed you'd be capable of. Your dirty talk has unlocked the door to all sorts of experiences you didn't know how to ask for, and you'll enjoy some a lot more than others.

I also recommend checking out my book, _The Temptress's Handbook_, if you're looking for even more ways to seduce your man and keep his attention firmly on you. It's packed with tips for a spicier love life, from kissing and foreplay to the positions that will make both of you scream out with pleasure.

But for now, as you lay there, spent and content, with your honey by your side, it's a great time to ask him how he felt about whatever particular experience you just tried out together. If both of you found it truly exhilarating, agree to try it again some time – but maybe only after you've explored a few more of your options first.

After all, with one of the most powerful sexual tools now freely available to you to use, what's stopping you from continuing this adventure for the rest of your life? Enjoy your newfound freedom, my friend – you've earned every last tingle you're going to feel.

Special Thanks

I would like to give special thanks to all the readers from around the globe who chose to share their kind and encouraging words with me.

Knowing even just one person found this book helpful means the world to me.

If you've benefited from this book at all, I would be honored to have you share your thoughts on it, so that others would get something valuable out of this book as well.

Your reviews are the fuel for my writing soul, and I'd be **<u>forever grateful</u>** to see *your* review, too.

Thank you all.

9 781456 637194